ARCHAEOLOGY

and

WETHERBURN'S TAVERN

Colonial Williamsburg Archaeological Series No. 3

ARCHAEOLOGY *and* WETHERBURN'S TAVERN

by

IVOR NOËL HUME

Published by
THE COLONIAL WILLIAMSBURG FOUNDATION
Williamsburg, Virginia

ISBN 0-910412-08-1
LC No. 76-84024
Second printing, 1976
Printed in the United States of America

PREFACE

The results of the excavations at Wetherburn's Tavern are typical of the kind of information recovered from most archaeologically explored sites in Williamsburg. For that reason this project has been chosen as the first of its kind to be published in Colonial Williamsburg's archaeological series. It is to be hoped that this account of what was found and how the archaeological, architectural, and historical evidence fused together to arrive at final conclusions will give the reader some idea of the kinds of reasoning that must be applied to the interpretation of any colonial site.

For the benefit of those who may wish to use the illustrated artifacts for comparative purposes or who need to cite them as parallels in their own publications, the catalog number and measurements of each item are listed on pages 46 and 47.

I.N.H.

December 1968.

ARCHAEOLOGY
and
WETHERBURN'S
TAVERN

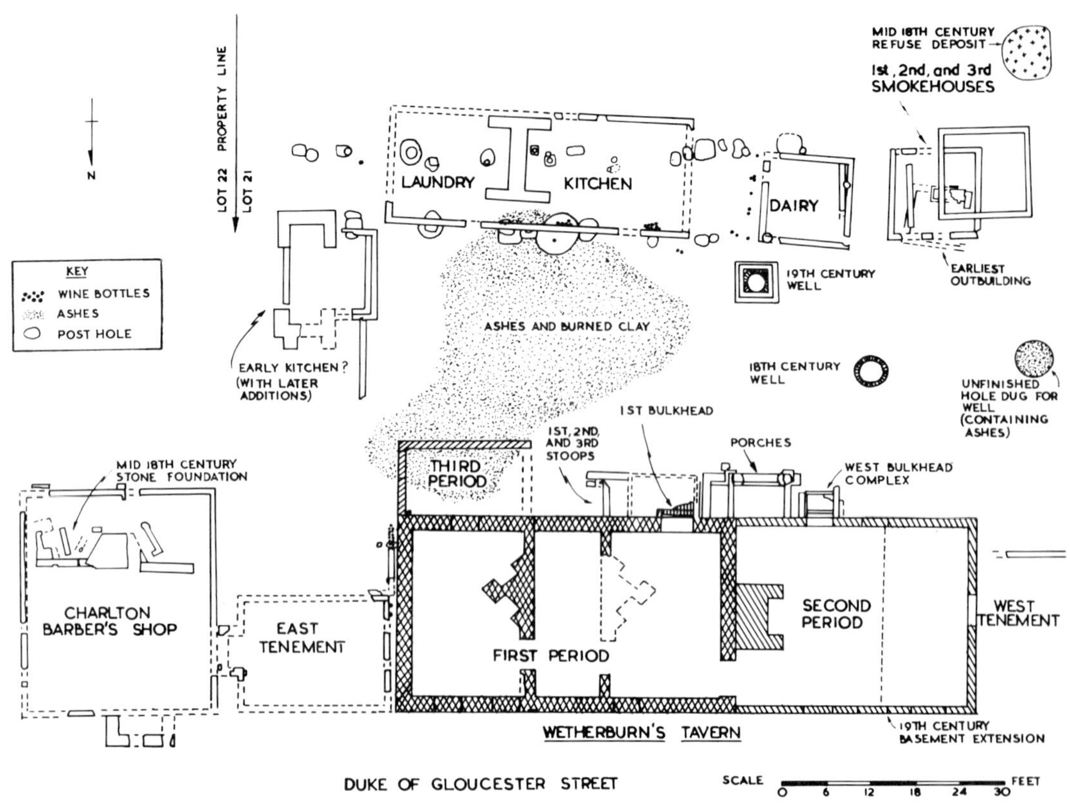

FRONTISPIECE:

Plan of Wetherburn's Tavern and the principal archaeological features associated with it.

Many people think of archaeology as being applicable only to sites where buildings have disappeared or, at best, have been reduced to picturesque ruins. This is quite wrong, and the excavations at Wetherburn's Tavern graphically demonstrated how much the archaeologist's trowel can tell us about the life and history of an existing building.

Standing as it does on the south side of Duke of Gloucester Street, only 250 yards from the Capitol, Wetherburn's Tavern was one of Williamsburg's principal colonial hostelries. It remains today among the town's most impressive original, semipublic buildings. In the eighteenth century the tavern's fame was such that the quality of other establishments was measured against it. In 1775 merchant Daniel Fisher described the ordinary at Leeds Town as having "as elegant an appearance as any I have seen in the country, Mr. Finnays or Wetherbernes in Williamsburg not excepted." Mr. Finney was the proprietor of the renowned Raleigh Tavern across the street from Wetherburn's establishment.

Colonial lots 20 and 21, whereon Wetherburn's Tavern stands, were acquired by Colonial Williamsburg under long-term lease in 1964, and the first steps were quickly taken toward restoring the property to its colonial appearance. These began, as all such programs must, with a thorough study of the documentary history. Researchers pursued every reference to the tavern or to its successive owners from the day in 1716 when Richard Bland, the first recorded owner of the property, conveyed the lots to Colonel

Nathaniel Harrison, through to 1964 when Mrs. Virginia Bruce Haughwout leased them to Colonial Williamsburg.

No one knew exactly when the tavern was built, but plainly it had seen many structural changes during its two hundred and more years of life. It was hoped that they could be dated through the study of the historical, the architectural, or the archaeological evidence. Archaeological reasoning is most often based on the relationships of artifacts and foundations to the layers of the ground in which they are buried. At Wetherburn's Tavern, however, the archaeology began in the roof and continued down into the basement. The alteration of chimneys, the replastering of walls—and even the remodeling activities of rats and squirrels—had resulted in the burial of artifacts in the dust and debris behind laths and between floor joists. When uncovered, many of the artifacts provided clues to the dates when the "improvements" occurred. Among the treasures recovered were pieces of leather shoes, fragments of pottery and glass, a brass button, a miniature padlock (*Figure 1*), large numbers of nails, and even larger quantities of squirrel-secreted nuts and rat-gnawed chicken bones.

It was immediately apparent that the tavern grew in three stages. The primary structure lay to the east and possessed four rooms on the first floor, a central passage, and two triangular-based chimneys (only one of which survived). The whole measured approximately forty-five feet by twenty-six feet. To this was added the "Great Room," extending the building thirty-two feet to the west. The third phase of the tavern's evolution comprised

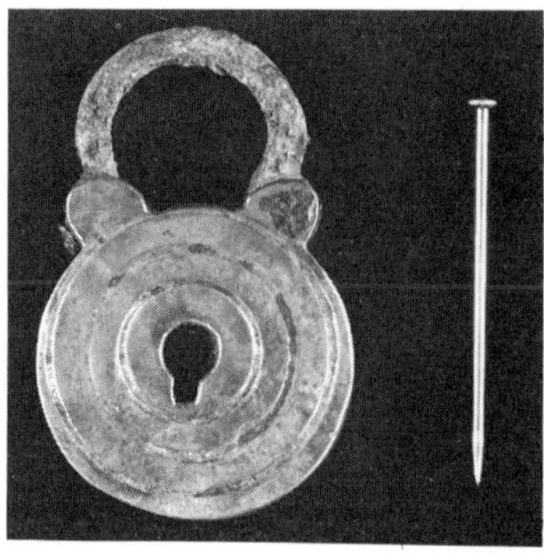

FIGURE 1
Miniature brass padlock, perhaps for a jewel box or a dog collar. Found behind the lath-and-plaster wall of the middle room; second half of eighteenth century. The pin measures one inch.

the building of a small shed-roofed extension to the southeast corner of the primary unit.

Full-scale archaeological excavations began in the spring of 1965 and were initially confined to attempts to determine the dates when the second and third sections were appended to the tavern and to locating the remains of early porches and entrances into the basement. The southeasterly extension had no basement, and there was hope that layers predating its construction would survive beneath it *(Figure 2)*. What was not immediately apparent was the fact that throughout the nineteenth century occupants of the building had thrown their trash under the extension, presumably shoveling it through a window opening in the wall of the first period basement. Most of this material consisted of bones, broken pottery and glass, and pieces of shoes, the bulk of it dating from the second quarter of the nineteenth century.

FIGURE 2
Archaeological work in progress beneath the floor of the tavern's southeast addition.

FIGURE 3
A motion picture record of the archaeological work was kept as digging progressed along the south face of the tavern.

Beneath the rubbish, and of much more importance, was a layer of brick rubble and ashes that extended away from the tavern, passing beneath the foundations of the shed addition. Evidently, therefore, the layer was older than the foundation, and it remained for the artifacts recovered from the ashes to reveal how old. The answer was somewhere around 1750, although the excavators could not be sure whether that meant 1745 or 1755, or perhaps even a little later. Closer dating would eventually be possible, but it was not forthcoming until nearly eighteen months later and from digging on the far side of the property.

The architectural restoration of the tavern involved the removal of a late porch and a modern bulkhead entrance to the basement at the north, as well as the dismantling of a large screen porch along the south face of the building. Digging beneath the screen porch revealed two separate locations for bulkheads, a nineteenth-century root cellar, and the remains of no fewer than five stoops, two in one location and three in another (*Figure 3*). The difficulty was to determine which were in use contemporaneously and at the date to which the tavern was to be restored.

The decision as to the date was dictated by the fact that Henry Wetherburn died in 1760, and the inventory made at that time identified the various rooms and provided precedent for the furnishings to be used in them. None of the subsequent owners or operators of the tavern was as well known as Wetherburn, and they left no inventories describing the building's contents during their occupancy. Consequently, the archaeologist's principal task was to determine which structures and artifacts dated from the Wetherburn period and which did not.

Most of the bulkheads and porches along the south face of the tavern proved not to be of the right date, and consequently they have not been reconstructed. Nevertheless, the investigation of one predominantly later complex provided a classic example of archaeological detection. Digging beside the southwest entrance to the tavern the excavators came upon a bricked-in entrance to the basement below the "Great Room." The brick steps leading down to it had been covered by a thick layer of clay, while the entrance

FIGURE 4a
The bricked-in southwest bulkhead entrance revealed after the removal of fill sealing the steps.

itself had been sealed with bricks salvaged from a chimney *(Figure 4a)*. That this was their source was indicated by the coating of soot still adhering to some that had been used in the interior of the flue. The bricks proved to be of the same size and color as those used in the foundation of the surviving triangular chimney to the east of the tavern's entrance passage. It could be deduced, therefore, that when the companion chimney to the west of the passage was dismantled, some of the bricks were used to seal up the west bulkhead. The all-important question was: When did these changes occur? The answer came from a fragment of pottery found in the clay fill over the bulkhead steps, clay that was undoubtedly inserted immediately after the entrance was bricked in. The pottery proved to be a fragment of English transfer-printed pearlware manufactured around 1820.

FIGURE 4b
The same entrance after reopening the doorway and removing the later eighteenth-century steps to expose the remains of an earlier set beneath.

The first rule of archaeology is that you date each layer by the most recent artifact found in it. This is known as a *terminus post quem*, the date after which the most recent artifact was thrown away. It can, of course, be *any* date after, but it cannot be before. Thus, the clay burying the bulkhead steps could not have been deposited before about 1820, and as the clay was placed there within days or hours after the entrance was bricked up, it followed that the chimney from which the bricks came was being taken down at approximately the same date.

When the bricked-up entrance was reopened, it was found that an earlier approach to it had been sealed beneath the last brick steps. These in turn were duly removed, disclosing the debris from an earlier and largely robbed set of steps (*Figure 4b*). Here again, a fragment of pottery provided invaluable dating evidence. A sherd

FIGURE 5
After completion of work beneath the tavern's modern porch, attention was turned to the outbuildings. The foundations of a dairy are partially revealed to the left and those of the kitchen to the right.

of English creamware (often called Queen's Ware) was found in the filling between the early and late steps. This ware first appears in surviving Virginia records in 1769, and therefore it is reasonable to conclude that the upper set of steps was built after that date—long after the death of Henry Wetherburn. Consequently, the lower set has been reconstructed.

Once the chronology of the bulkheads and porches had been established, the archaeological digging was extended southward across the tavern yard toward the inevitable outbuildings, outbuildings that were shown on a 1782 map of the city, and all but one of which had long since disappeared. The surviving structure proved to have been a frame smokehouse that had been converted from an earlier dairy and that, having been adapted to modern usage, was now seated on a twentieth-century brick footing.

Digging both inside and outside the smokehouse revealed the mutilated foundations of three previous structures, two of them smokehouses, and one (the earliest) of unknown purpose. Another foundation of a size comparable to that of the smokehouse lay some seven feet to the east, and as no firebox was found, it was deduced that this had been a dairy. Consequently, because the surviving frame smokehouse had begun life as a dairy, Colonial Williamsburg architects concluded that it had originally stood on these footings. It has therefore been moved back onto them and restored to its dairy period (*see Figure 37*).

Less than ten feet to the east of the dairy the foundations of a large kitchen building were uncovered, a building having two rooms on the first floor with a massive H-shaped chimney between them (*Figure 5*). In all, the story-and-a-half structure had measured approximately forty feet by twenty feet, and its hearths had been more than eight feet in width. The ash and burned brick previously encountered beneath the tavern's southeast shed extended up to the kitchen's north foundation and stopped on that line, except for one small patch that projected beyond the wall and reached almost to the foundation of the chimney. It was apparent, therefore, that the burned debris had not come from the destruction of the kitchen, but was deposited before the building was erected. On the other hand, the fact that it stopped on the line of the kitchen could not have been entirely coincidental. As so frequently happens in archaeology, the removal of one soil layer asks the questions, and digging through another provides the answers. In this case, careful scraping alongside the north wall of the kitchen revealed that it rested on a series of dirt-filled holes. These had almost certainly housed the posts for a fence that had been taken down when the kitchen was built (*Figure 6*).

The discovery of the fenceline explained why the burned debris was confined to the area north of the kitchen, but there was still no explanation as to whence it came, and no very firm date after which the fire must have occurred. One important fact did emerge; the ashes and brick rubble were not from a fire that

FIGURE 6
Large roots had done considerable damage to the kitchen's north foundation. Behind it lies the footing for the large H-shaped chimney.

occurred on some other Williamsburg property, for the ground beneath was locally scorched, indicating that the ashes were hot when they first rested on it. It was also clear that the fire had been of considerable intensity, burning white salt-glazed stoneware black, warping porcelain, melting wine glasses, medicine bottles, and even brass buckles. However, the most important questions still remained: What burned, and when?

The investigation of the north foundation for the kitchen not only revealed the row of post holes, it also produced another surprise, no fewer than eighteen glass bottles buried in units of three, five, and ten, with a post hole between each group (*Figure 7*). The construction of the kitchen foundations had missed the

FIGURE 7
Ten bottles, some containing cherries, and all dating from the 1740s, were found near the northwest corner of the kitchen. They are seen here before being removed from the ground.

necks of the bottles by inches, but three more buried on the same line between kitchen and dairy were less fortunate. All three had had their necks broken by subsequent gardening or grading. The row of bottles that had run east-to-west beside the colonial fence did not continue beneath the dairy, but turned abruptly southward along its east face. A single bottle was found at the northeast and southeast corners, another more or less in the middle, and groups of two and three on either side of it. There could be no doubt that all these bottles were buried for the same purpose and presumably at much the same time, probably in the mid-eighteenth century, as the latest of the bottle shapes could not have dated before 1750.

Three more intact bottles were found outside the north wall of the kitchen, two of them together and on their sides, and it is reasonable to contend that all were part of the same bottle-burying project. The most easterly group of three bottles *(Figure 8)*, from beneath and inside the kitchen wall, were different from all the others; they were wide-mouthed and were of a type used to store bottled fruit. There was none in them. The next group westward included one French wine bottle along with four English examples of the 1740s, and these, too, were empty. The bottles in the largest group, just inside the northwest corner of the kitchen, were also English and of the same date, but differed in that they were not empty.

The majority of the bottles were more than half full of an unattractive brown liquid, plus quantities of cherry pits, cut stems, and in some cases intact cherries. Laboratory examination of the liquid revealed no alcoholic content, but the cherries were determined to be of the English black Morello variety, and each had had its stem trimmed approximately a quarter of an inch from the fruit. While Colonial Williamsburg's archaeological and research staffs were puzzling over how to explain this strange discovery, a cache of fifteen more bottles was found in a trench north of the shed addition (*Figures 9 and 10*). Many of these bottles contained the same reddish-brown liquid, but more cherries than had been recovered from those under the kitchen.

Some of the bottles had had wet clay wrapped over the corks, and although the corks themselves had all shrunk and had dropped inside, the clay kept the contents safe from contamination by the dirt above them. However, it did not prevent the contents from slowly evaporating or the rain water falling from the tavern's eaves from percolating down into the bottles. Because they were found to contain intact cherries at the bottoms and only pits above, it was deduced that the liquid level rose and fell through the years, causing those cherries that protruded above it to decay, while those below were preserved. In one instance the bottle was cracked and nothing, not even the pits, remained inside, demonstrating that if the fruit remained dry for any length of time even the pits would be destroyed. This doubtless accounted for the widely differing numbers of pits and cherries recovered from the

FIGURE 8

Wide-mouthed green glass bottles of unusual shapes found together beneath the kitchen's north wall. The two squat examples are rare and have a body shape that normally dates before 1725, while the taller octagonal example was made in the period 1740–1760.

FIGURE 9

Fifteen bottles were found in a group beside the tavern's southeast corner, many of them still retaining both cherries and liquid. The bottles are of shapes made in the period 1735–1745. The paper stoppers, replacing rotted or shrunken corks, were inserted by the excavators to prevent evaporation or dirt falling into the contents.

FIGURE 10
The fifteen bottles after treatment.

FIGURE 11
The contents of the bottles were carefully extracted in the laboratory.

various intact bottles, the counts ranging from 72 to 249 (*Figures 11 and 12*). The simple laboratory experiment of taking 249 modern cherries of the same size and pushing them into the bottle revealed that virtually no room remained for the addition of liquid, thus raising the possibility that the original cherries were bottled dry. However, the experiment also yielded another informational gem: once in, the modern cherries could not be extracted intact.

Eighteenth- and nineteenth-century documentary sources contributed various scraps of seemingly relevant data, but no one of them exactly described all the features of the Wetherburn

FIGURE 12
Examples of cherries from the Wetherburn Tavern bottles were preserved in plastic, clearly revealing that the stalks had been trimmed before the fruit was placed in the bottles.

FIGURE 13
A half-gallon bottle now in the refurnished tavern, dated 1738 and paralleling one buried beside the east wall.

FIGURE 12

FIGURE 13

discovery. The practice of burying bottles was vouched for in the 1753 Supplement to Ephraim Chambers's *Cyclopaedia*, whose essay on bottling offered the following:

> Something also depends on the place where the bottles are set, which ought to be such as exposes them as little as possible to the alterations and impressions of the air: the ground is better for this purpose than a frame, sand better than the bare ground, and a running water, or a spring often changed, best of all.

Evidence for the cutting of the cherries' stems before putting them in the bottles came from a recipe for "Brandy Cherries" in a manuscript cookbook compiled in Virginia in 1836:

> Select the nicest Cherries, trim them, leaving a short Stem to each Cherry that the juice may be retained. Wash and wipe them gently and put them in large-mouthed Bottles. Have ready a good syrup (a pint of Water to a Pound of Sugar) and when it is nearly cold add one Pint and a Half of French Brandy to every Pint of Syrup [,] mix it thoroughly and pour it cold over yr. Cherries. Seal the Bottles well.

The Wetherburn cherries had been trimmed, a short stem was left, and three of the bottles were wide mouthed, but neither sugar nor brandy was present in the surviving liquid. That cherries were bottled dry was proved by an entry in the diary of William Byrd of Westover; on November 7, 1709, he stayed with his cousin Edmund Berkeley at Barn Elms in Middlesex County.

> His wife was at home and gave us a good supper. I ate boiled beef. Then we had some cherries which had been scalded in hot water which did not boil and then put in bottles without water in them. They were exceedingly good.

Cherry brandy, brandied cherries, or bottled cherries? There are arguments for and against each possibility. Unless some additional evidence comes to light, we can do no better than to bring in the old Scottish verdict of "Not Proven." However, one fact is indisputable; this is the largest collection of intact bottles yet recovered from any Williamsburg excavation.

FIGURE 14a
Foot and support fragments from a small brass smoker's brazier or chafing dish were among the many metal artifacts found near the tavern. The pin measures one inch.

FIGURE 14b
A brazier paralleling the excavated fragments, now in the refurnished tavern. Mid-eighteenth century.

FIGURE 14a

FIGURE 14b

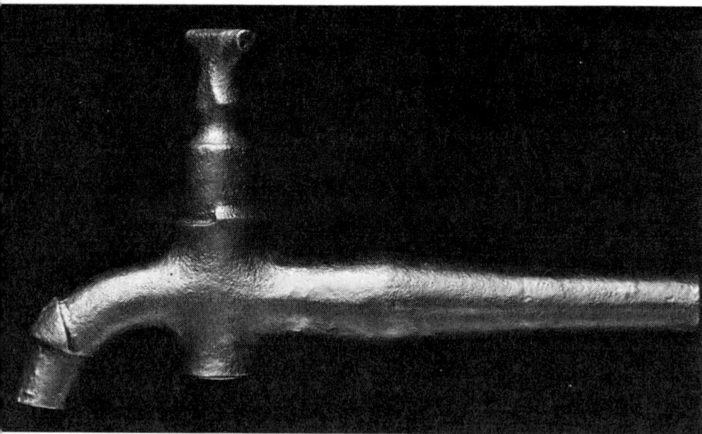

FIGURE 15
A copper alloy spiggot for tapping a barrel, found near the East Tenement. Eighteenth century.

FIGURE 16
Brass candlesticks and snuffers found to the rear of the tavern. The stick to the left was probably manufactured in the period 1695–1710, and that to the right between 1715 and 1740. The latter, and the two pairs of snuffers, seem to have been discarded before the mid-century fire.

FIGURE 17

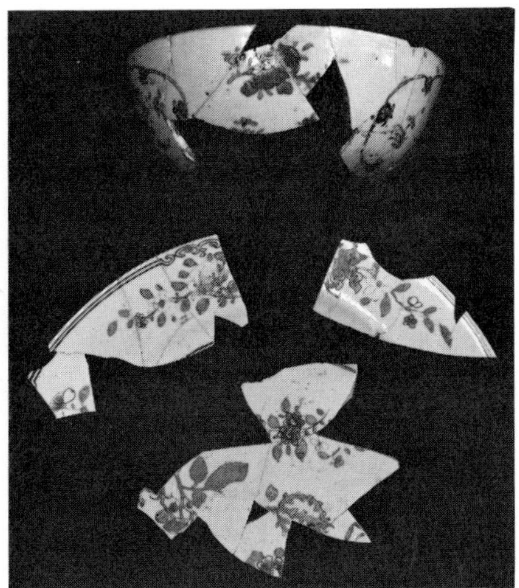

FIGURE 18

FIGURE 17
Grey stoneware mug with incised and cobalt-painted decoration and medallion. Made in the Westerwald district of the Rhineland, this example is unusual in that it is of "6" or pint capacity. Mid-eighteenth century.

FIGURE 18
Bowl and plate fragments of Chinese export porcelain decorated in overglaze green, red, pink, and black, and paralleling the set of "white flowered China" listed in Henry Wetherburn's inventory of 1760. These and many more fragments were found in the yard to the rear of the tavern.

There was no shortage of other artifacts; in fact, more than 200,000 fragments of pottery, glass, and metal objects were recovered during the two seasons' work. Most of the pieces were small and were recovered from the yard metaling behind the tavern, where they had been rolled into the ground along with oyster shells and brickbats to provide a durable surface. While every effort was made to put the bowls, cups, plates, and bottles together again, the results were unspectacular. Nevertheless, from an archaeological rather than a museum point of view, a single fragment can be as useful as a complete item. Thus, for example, scattered fragments of Chinese export porcelain decorated with overglaze flowers in red, pink, and green could be equated with the "1 set white flowered China" listed in the 1760 inventory of Henry Wetherburn's estate *(Figure 18)*.

FIGURE 19a

Rim fragments from a white saltglaze plate decorated with a portrait of Frederick, King of Prussia, an eagle, a battle trophy, and the slogan "SUCCESS TO THE KING OF PRUSSIA AND HIS FORCES." *Such plates were made during the Seven Years' War (1756–1763) capitalizing on the popularity of Frederick the Great after the victory at Rossbach in 1757. Fragments of two other such plates were found in the Wetherburn Tavern excavations.*

FIGURE 19b

An intact "King of Prussia" white saltglaze plate now in the refurnished tavern, and made from the same mold block as the excavated examples. About 1760.

FIGURE 20
A mid-eighteenth-century rubbish deposit in course of excavation to the south of the Wetherburn smokehouse complex.

In addition to the artifacts found in the yard metaling, a more concentrated group of larger pieces was found in a shallow depression south of the smokehouse *(Figure 20)*. These dated from the mid-eighteenth century and included nineteen wine glass stems, one of them of a rare type dating from the late seventeenth century *(Figure 21)*. The same deposit yielded the glass seal from a wine bottle bearing the initials "ID," which may be those of John Doncastle, a tavern-keeper who rented "the House of Mr. Wetherburn" from 1753 to 1755.

Abandoned and trash-filled well shafts are potentially the most productive and informative of all archaeological features encountered on a colonial site, and therefore it was disappointing to find that an old well remained open when the property was acquired by Colonial Williamsburg *(see Figure 5)*. Such wells have invariably been cleaned out many times in the course of their lives and therefore contain little of any antiquity. The only hope lay in the possibility that the one used by Wetherburn had been filled and was concealed somewhere on the site. There was much excitement when a circular hole five feet in diameter (the usual exterior diameter for a brick-lined well shaft) was found close to the west property line. Although none of the brickwork remained, the vertical sides of the hole left little doubt that it was, indeed, a well

FIGURE 21
Examples of wine glass stems from various locations on the Wetherburn site. Top row: *(1–3) inverted baluster and knopped stems, ca. 1695–1720; (4) acorn-knopped stem, ca. 1700–1720; (5) stem topped by a mushroom knop, ca. 1705–1730.* Bottom row: *(6) molded Silesian stem with diamond-shaped bosses at the shoulders, ca. 1715–1730; (7) drawn stem with elongated tear, ca. 1725–1745; (8) straight stem with central angular knop, ca. 1730–1750; (9) solid stem with elongated, inverted baluster and knop above the foot, ca. 1725–1750; (10) drawn stem with air twist decoration, ca. 1735–1755; (11) straight stem with opaque-twist ornament, a pair of corkscrew tapes around a central gauze, ca. 1755–1770.*

shaft. Artifacts from the upper filling indicated that the bricks had been salvaged, and the hole filled, in the mid-eighteenth century. Consequently the excavators were deeply disappointed when the hole came to an abrupt halt only four feet six inches below the modern surface. So suddenly had the digging stopped that one could still see the impression of the spade blade in the clay where the colonial workman had been about to cut deeper. The only

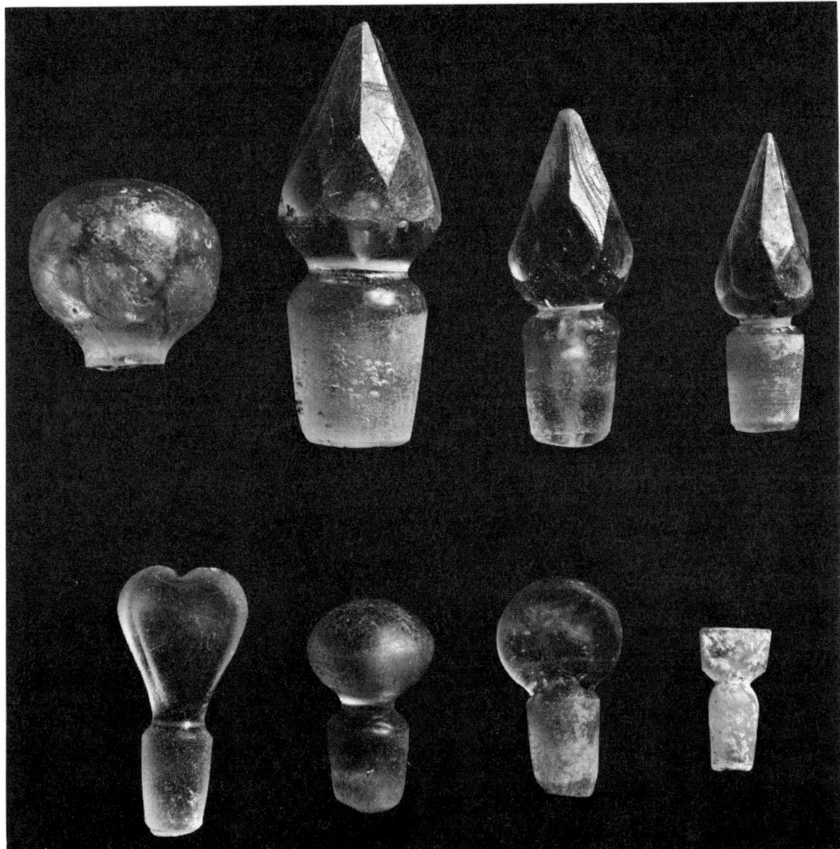

FIGURE 22
Lead-glass decanter and bottle stoppers found in the vicinity of the tavern. Top row: *(1) ball finial with multiple tears, ca. 1720–1750; (2–4) faceted steeple-finialed stoppers, ca. 1750–1775.* Bottom row: *(5) heart-shaped finial; (6) flattened ball finial; (7) disc finial; (8) block finial, all of late eighteenth- or early nineteenth-century date.*

reasonable explanation must be that he had stopped when told that he was sinking it in the wrong place.

The shaft, which thereafter became known as the "abortive well," had been filled with clay and, at the bottom, with a quantity of wood ashes and brickbats. Numerous pieces of pottery and glass were retrieved from the ashes, among them fragments of pharmaceutical phials that had melted in a fire and resembled those found in the mysterious burned layer under the tavern's southeast extension. However, the most important item from the "abortive well" proved to be a small clear glass bottle shaped rather like a cello and embossed with the following inscription: ROB^{T} TURLINGTON^{S} BALSAM OF LIFE BY THE KINGS PATENT MARCH 25 1750 *(Figure 24).* As the bottle could not have been made before 1750, it could be reasoned that the well-digging operation was going on no earlier than the summer of that year. This conclusion, like most archaeological reasoning, calls for no more than simple common sense.

Robert Turlington's balsam was too popular and in 1754 he designed a new bottle in an effort to defeat pirates who were copying both his product and its container. The post-1754 bottles are well known and easily recognized, but before the discovery of Mr. Wetherburn's "abortive well," no example of the 1750 bottle was known to survive. Indeed, no one realized that the pre-1754 bottle had been of a distinctive type, and for this reason two fragments previously found in the burned layer north of the kitchen were not recognized for what they were. However, when the complete bottle was recovered, there was no doubt that the pieces came from bottles of the same type. Thus it could be unequivocally proved that the fire occurred after March 1750, while the presence of the same kind of debris in the well indicated that the shaft was being dug after the fire was over.

If the first well shaft was dug in the wrong place, it had to be followed by another in the right one—and it was. A second, filled shaft of the same diameter was found seventeen feet to the east. It, too, had been robbed of its brick lining, but only to a depth of fifteen feet. The upper levels had been filled with domestic refuse in the late eighteenth century, apparently after the filling below

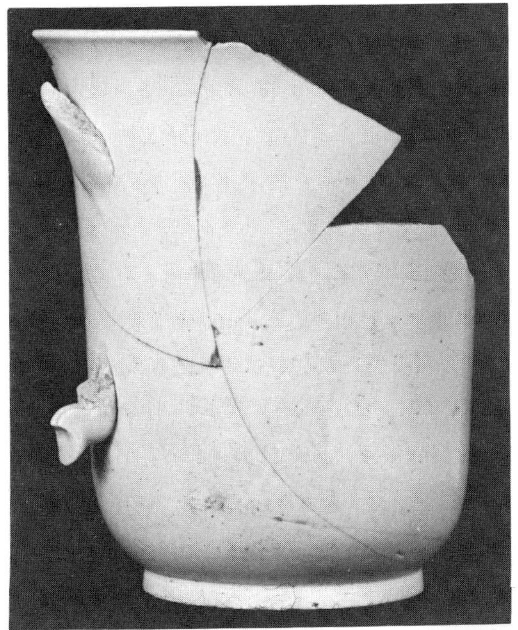

FIGURE 23
White salt-glazed stoneware cup or capuchine found in the unfinished well shaft. Second quarter of the eighteenth century.

FIGURE 24
Bottle of clear lead glass bearing the molded inscription "ROB^{T}. TURLINGTON^{S}. BALSAM OF LIFE BY THE KINGS PATENT MARCH 25 1750," *decorated below the neck on one side with a crude rendering of the British royal arms and their supporters and on the other with a shield bearing three pear-shaped devices. This bottle was found in the filling of the unfinished well shaft.*

FIGURE 25
The principal eighteenth-century well shaft in the process of excavation. The upper courses of the brick lining had been salvaged when the well was abandoned. The archaeologists were forced to replace the missing and damaged brickwork to a depth of twenty feet with steel conduit, which can be seen to end where the surviving brick wall begins. The wooden frame serves to hold the bricks in position and to prevent them from being dislodged when the excavators' buckets are hauled past the edge.

settled. At nineteen feet from the top, in a layer of ashes, were found two medicine bottles (one of them still corked, sealed with wax, and retaining most of its contents), a broken wine glass, and the body of a small and elaborately engraved decanter inscribed "MADEIRA" *(Figures 26 and 27)*. The technique of engraving the name of the proposed contents on the decanter in a cartouche resembling a silver wine label became fashionable in the mid-eighteenth century. An advertisement in the *Mercury* of Norwich, England, for December 26, 1755, listed "new fashioned decanters with inscriptions engraven on them, Port, Claret, Mountain, etc., etc." They were being sold in New York nine years later when the New York *Gazette, or Weekly Post-Boy* was advertising "new fashioned decanters labeled Madeira."

FIGURE 26

FIGURE 27

FIGURE 26
One of two clear lead-glass medicine phials found in the well filling at a depth of nineteen feet. This example retains its cork and some of the sealing wax as well as half its contents. About 1765.

FIGURE 27
Miniature label decanter engraved MADEIRA, *the best preserved example of wheel engraving excavated in Williamsburg. Found at a depth of nineteen feet in the tavern well. About 1760.*

FIGURE 28
Examples of the many fruit pits, vegetable seeds, and nuts recovered from the well, which provided precedent for details of the reconstructed yard and kitchen garden.

Well shafts generally become interesting once one reaches the water level, for below that point there is a good chance that objects of wood, textile, leather, and even paper will be preserved. The water level in Mr. Wetherburn's well was reached at a depth of twenty-two feet, but the next three feet failed to yield anything very spectacular. At twenty-five feet the fill became more muddy and began to give up pieces of twigs, nuts, and even seeds, important evidence to be used by the landscape architects in restoring the tavern's yard and kitchen gardens *(Figure 28)*.

Once the excavators reach the water it is necessary for every bucketful of dirt, and even of water, to be carefully strained so that not even the smallest grape pit is lost. In the Wetherburn well some of the pottery was broken up almost that small, and a rare green-glazed plate decorated with fruit in relief was found broken into fifty-two pieces and scattered through five feet of mud (*Figure 29a*). All save two small pieces were retrieved, thus

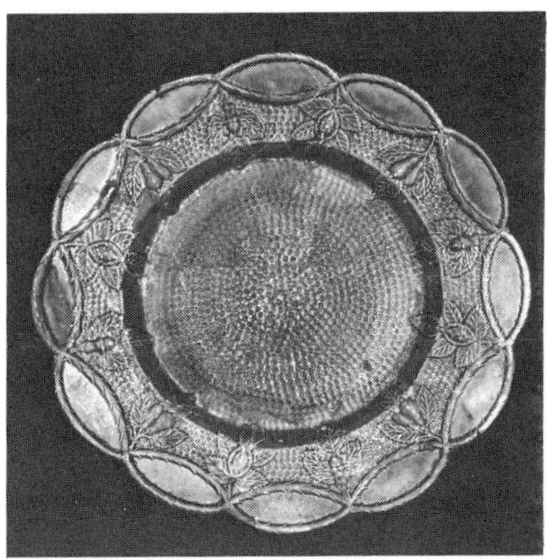

FIGURE 29a

FIGURE 29b

FIGURE 29a
A green-glazed cream-colored earthenware plate decorated with relief-molded fruit, the glaze developed by Josiah Wedgwood in 1759, and the shape cast from a mold originally designed for shaping white saltglaze. About 1760–1765. The many fragments of the plate were found scattered through the lower levels of the filled tavern well.

FIGURE 29b
A comparable plate presented to Colonial Williamsburg after the tavern example was found.

providing the first virtually complete example to be found in Williamsburg. Although the design is rare, pieces from four comparable plates were found on the site, suggesting that the rarity results more from the small number made than from any high contemporary value.

Other artifacts recovered from the lower filling of the well included leather shoes (*Figure 30*), fragments of twill woven in brown and fawn, perhaps from a blanket (*Figure 31*), a wooden-handled adze believed to have been used to salvage bricks from the well lining (*Figure 32*), and most important of all, the well bucket and a length of chain that had been attached to it. The oak-staved bucket was squashed flat under quantities of brickbats, but careful laboratory treatment restored it to its original appearance (*Figure 33*). When full it weighed sixty pounds and that, plus the weight of the chain, called for winding gear more substantial than the simple pulley wheel to be seen in most Williamsburg wellheads. The discovery therefore provided precedent for the use of a windlass, while the reconstruction is based on an intact example at the nearby George Reid House (*Figures 34a and b*).

Unfortunately, owing to the unstable condition of the well's lower brick courses, digging had to be abandoned before the last

FIGURE 30
Children's and adults' shoes found in the lower filling of the tavern well, all discarded before about 1770. The center example exhibits a contemporary patch on the side of the upper.

FIGURE 31
A fragment of twill woven from brown and beige threads and found in the wet filling of the tavern well. It is seen here over a blanket of similar color and weave from Colonial Williamsburg's Department of Collections that is now included in the tavern furnishings.

FIGURE 32

FIGURE 32
A scrubbing brush and an oak-handled adze, both found below the water level in the filled tavern well. The wood-backed brush still retains its worn hog bristles; between them were found strands of horsehair, suggesting that it was used for grooming. The adze is believed to have been used to dismantle the upper courses of the brick-lined shaft and to have been broken in the process. Both date before about 1770.

FIGURE 33
The oak bucket from the tavern well, the staves reassembled and the rusted iron hoops replaced. The pile of chain at right was used in hauling it, the toggle bolt being needed to prevent the links from becoming twisted as the bucket rotated. Both bucket and chain were found in the lower filling of the well shaft and so date before about 1770.

FIGURE 33

FIGURE 34a
The Wetherburn's Tavern wellhead after reconstruction. The style was dictated by the discovery of the very large and heavy bucket and the chain that supported it, indicating that a winch was needed in addition to the usual block. The exactly reproduced bucket and chain can be seen in the doorway.

FIGURE 34b
An original winch-operated wellhead at the nearby George Reid House that provided precedent for the Wetherburn reconstruction.

of the filling had been extracted. However, groping below the water and amid the brick rubble yielded an intact wine bottle dating from about 1750–1760 along with a blacking or snuff bottle of much the same date *(Figure 35)*. This evidence, coupled with that from further up the shaft, strongly suggested that the well had been abandoned and filled around 1765 or 1770.

Just as the excavators never quite reached the bottom of the well so they failed to get to the bottom of all the mysteries of Henry Wetherburn's tavern. Why were the cherry-filled bottles buried in the yard, and why did their owner never retrieve them? Where was the well that served the property before the "abortive" shaft was dug in the 1750s, and what was the origin of the ashes and burned debris that were so liberally strewn between tavern

FIGURE 35
Glass snuff and wine bottles found at the bottom of the eighteenth-century tavern well. Both about 1750–1760.

FIGURE 36
Foundations of the tavern's kitchen and adjacent outbuildings at the conclusion of the first season's digging.

and kitchen, and, finally, where was the kitchen that must have existed before the mid-eighteenth-century building was erected?

Some people wonder why archaeology plays any part in the study of a period as recent as the eighteenth century. After all, they contend, there are written records to tell us all we need to know. For those skeptics, the story of this Williamsburg tavern serves to demonstrate how quickly time mutilates even recent history—and not all the archaeologists or all the historians can put every piece of it together again.

FIGURE 37
Wetherburn's Tavern yard and outbuildings after restoration and reconstruction.

*Figure**		*Colonial Williamsburg catalog number*	*Measurements*
1.		5029. E.R.1000F–9.N.	Diam. 13/16″
7.		5044–5054. E.R.1029F–9.N.	Hts. range from 7 3/4″ – 9 1/8″
8, No.	1.	3980. E.R.1016C–9.N.	Ht. 5 1/2″
	2.	3981. E.R.1016C–9.N.	Ht. 8″
	3.	3982. E.R.1016C–9.N.	Ht. 6″
10.		5030–5044. E.R.1043D–9.N.	Hts. range from 7 1/2″ – 9 3/4″
12, No.	1.	5039. E.R.1043D–9.N.	Ht. 9″
	2.	5032. E.R.1043D–9.N.	Ht. 8″
13.		1968 – 108	Ht. 9 13/16″
14a, No.	1.	5026. E.R.1012D–9.N.	Ht. 1″
	2.	5024. E.R.1009E–9.N.	Ht. 1 1/16″
	3.	5025. E.R.1020D–9.N.	Ht. 1 1/8″
14b.		1952 – 106	Ht. 3 3/4″
15.		5027. E.R.1052B–9.P.	Length 6 1/4″
16, No.	1.	5020. E.R.1165G–9.N.	Ht. 5 1/4″
	2.	5021. E.R.1020K–9.N.	Ht. 6 1/4″
	3.	5022. E.R.1048H–9.N.	Length 5″
	4.	5023. E.R.1009E–9.N.	Length 5 3/8″
17.		5066. E.R.1030D–F, 1008K, 1009D–9.N.	Ht. 5″
18, No.	1.	5026. E.R.1009M,S–9.N.	Diam. 5 1/4″
	2.	5067. E.R.1025B, 1023A–9.N.	Diam. 10″
19a, No.	1.	3571a. E.R.1011B, 1030D–9.N.	Fragments from plates of approximately 9″ diameter.
	2.	3571b. E.R.1116–9.N.	
	3.	3572b. E.R.1012D,1157E–9.N.	
	4.	3570d. E.R.1030E, 1030L–9.N.	
	5.	3570c. E.R.1069C–9.N.	
19b.		1967 – 50	Diam. 9 5/16″
21, No.	1.	5055. E.R.1155R–9.P.	Ht. 3″
	2.	5056. E.R.1001D–9.N.	Ht. 3 3/8″

*Figure**	*Colonial Williamsburg catalog number*	*Measurements*
3.	5057. E.R.1183D–9.C.	Ht. 3 3/4″
4.	5059. E.R.1116C–9.N.	Ht. 3 5/8″
5.	5058. E.R.1004T–9.N.	Ht. 2 3/4″
6.	5060. E.R.1150A–9.N.	Ht. 4″
7.	5062. E.R.1165G–9.N.	Ht. 5″
8.	5061. E.R.1070–9.N.	Ht. 4 1/4″
9.	5063. E.R.1148F–9.N.	Ht. 4 1/4″
10.	5064. E.R.1011L–9.N.	Ht. 4 3/4″
11.	5065. E.R.1114C–9.P.	Ht. 3 3/4″
22, No. 1.	5070. E.R.1011D–9.N.	Ht. 1 1/4″
2.	5071. E.R.1123E–9.N.	Ht. 3 1/4″
3.	5073. E.R.1054B–9.N.	Ht. 2 1/2″
4.	5072. E.R.1070–9.N.	Ht. 2″
5.	5074. E.R.1145S–9.P.	Ht. 1 3/4″
6.	5073. E.R.1052B–9.P.	Ht. 1 3/4″
7.	5075. E.R.1004M–9.N.	Ht. 1 1/8″
23.	3359. E.R.1139A–B–9.N.	Ht. 3″
24.	3364. E.R.1139B–9.N.	Ht. 3 3/4″
26.	3763. E.R.1135–9.N.	Ht. 2 3/4″
27.	3403. E.R.1135F–9.N.	Ht. 2 3/4″
29a.	3385. E.R.1135R,S,T–9.N.	Diam. 9 1/4″
29b.	G1968 – 15	Diam. 8 11/16″
30, No. 1.	3784. E.R.1135Q–9.N.	Length 6 3/4″
2.	3785. E.R.1135S–9.N.	Length 7 1/2″
3.	3786. E.R.1135Q–9.N.	Length 9″
4.	3783. E.R.1135R–9.N.	Length 5″
31.	3438. E.R.1135R–9.N.	Length 9 1/2″
32, No. 1.	3405. E.R.1135R–9.N.	Length 10″
2.	3406. E.R.1135P–9.N.	Total length 2′9″
33.	3780. E.R.1135R–9.N.	Ht. 1′1 3/4″
35, No. 1.	3408. E.R.1135R–9.N.	Ht. 6 1/2″
2.	3407. E.R.1135T–9.N	Ht. 8″

* All numbering of multiple-item illustrations is from left to right and from top to bottom row.